Doing Business God's Way

❦

30 Devotions for the Entrepreneur

~ Francia Noble

Francia Noble

Printed in the United States of America

Let's Connect ...

༄

www.francianoble.com
www.facebook.com/francianoble
www.linkedin.com/francianoble
www.twitter.com/noblelifem
www.noblelifeministries.wordpress.com

This book is dedicated to three of the most beautiful yet "opinionated" people I have ever known:

My children… Jessica, William, and Jasmine

And to my friend, **Gladys Sykes,** *whom I know is looking down from Heaven saying,*
"It's about time."

Forward

One cannot imagine the number of times I have started a book only to be side-tracked for months or even years. So much time passes, experiences occur, and life in general moves onward before I have been able to put pen to paper again. The idea to write a book came to me as I was attending a conference on how to better my business and make money. Yet, when I sat down and began to brainstorm about my topic, I was led by that inner voice to produce something that might be helpful to people who would find themselves in a similar situation as me. The situation that I speak of is that of a serial entrepreneur.

I must tell you that not only am I a business person, I am also a child of God. I cannot recall a time in my life, except when I was being hard-headed, that I was not involved in church. As I grew, my relationship with the Father has grown. Out of that growth came the calling to be a minister of the gospel. I ran from that one for a long time. When I finally came to my senses, I told my best friend, Gladys. "What took you so long?!" she said. When I asked why she did not say anything, she reminded me that this was my journey and that I had to find my own way.

I am still finding my way, so to speak, and the journey has not always been an easy one. However, the Word of God reassures me that I can do all things through

Christ Jesus that strengthens me (Philippians 4:13).

Within these pages you will find scriptures, prayers, and personal anecdotes – motivation to be better than when you started. Over the next 30 days, I encourage you to use this devotional to create a shift in your business and your personal life. I pray that you will strengthen your relationship with God by spending time in His word and by spending time in prayer.

It is my hope that the Word of God combined with my thoughts will give you a sense of comfort, and the strength to continue the path of growing your business, all while not losing sight of WHO you are in Jesus Christ.

As an entrepreneur, I have experienced all of the joys and sorrows of trying to make it work. I have started and stopped many multi-level marketing businesses. I have been a business coach, event planner (social and professional), and officiated weddings. I have endured trials and tribulations. But through it all, the disappointments, the celebrations, and everything in between, God has blessed me. So I say to you...

Be Blessed!

EARLY TO RISE

"When you rise in the morning, give thanks for the light, for your life, for your strength. Give thanks for your food and for the joy of living.
If you see no reason to give thanks, the fault lies in yourself."

~ Tecumseh

Luke 21:38

*Then early in the morning
all the people came to Him
in the temple to hear Him.*

There is just something about the early morning hours, when the house is still quiet, that inspires me to be still and listen. It's that hour before all of the distractions of the outside world become so loud that no other voice can be heard, including my own; that quietness that lets me hear the beating of my chambered heart and hear every breath as it enters and leaves my body; that time when I can pick up my bible, read, pray, and hear the calmative voice of the one who made me.

As an entrepreneur, there are times when I am required to seek guidance from those who are far more knowledgeable and experienced in areas that I have not yet mastered nor have a desire to master. Yet, because of my mortal ways, I am leary of people I do not know. Fear grips me, as I seek out the assistance of others. As I assess what they may possess that will benefit my business, the wicked ways of the world attempt to persuade me to believe that everyone has an ulterior motive for wanting to help.

The Word of God tells us that we must continue to watch and be prayerful for the time will come when we will have to deal with those who are only seeking to destroy what we have worked to build. Yet, because of all of the messages running through our minds, we can misinterpret the true meaning of what we hear. These are times when we must turn to the almighty for his infinite wisdom in all things.

Lately, my moments of being watchful have been arriving at three o'clock in the morning. I wake to find that my mind is racing with thoughts of the previous day or to the many tasks that need to be accomplished within the next few hours. I find myself re-living the conversations I had or the new relationships that have been forged. As I am tossing and turning, I realize that it is all for nothing as the quiet still Voice of God reminds me that all is well and He is watching over me. It is at that moment that I begin to pray and eventually fall back into a peaceful sleep.

∽

Father in Heaven, in the still of this day, I thank you for the quiet reprieve that I am able to find in your Word. Lord, remove the outside distractions of this world so that I may be able to hear what I need to hear as I go about working my business. Allow me to actively listen as you guide me along this journey to all that you have purposed for my life and my business.

Amen

Lamentations 3:22-26

_____

*Through the Lord's mercies we are
not consumed, because His
compassions fail not.
They are new every morning;
great is Your faithfulness.
"The Lord is my portion,"
says my soul,
"Therefore I hope in Him!"
The Lord is good to those who wait
for Him, to the soul who seeks Him.*

*It is good that one should hope
and wait quietly for the
salvation of the Lord."*

Every day, is a new day in which you can experience God's compassion toward you. Rest assured that he has forgotten the mishaps of yesterday and has already extended to you His unfailing mercies.

With each new day you are given the opportunity to make a difference in the life of someone who does not have a relationship with the Lord. Rest easy in knowing that this does not mean that you have to recite scriptures or church doctrine. It does mean that you must share the love of Christ, even in your business dealings. How you treat others will be a blessing to you and to them. More importantly, the time you spend with them will restore a sense of hope in all of humanity that has been clouded by the selfishness of the world.

Every day you will encounter people who need what your business has to offer. Every day is a new day to hope and dream that you can accomplish the things you have only been thinking about.

God has given you the talent, the wisdom, and the knowledge to take your business to new heights if you only wait for HIM.

∽

My Heavenly Father, thank you for this new day. I am blessed to be given a new opportunity to bless those around me with the gifts that You have given unto me. I pray that as I conduct business today with my customers or clients that they will see Your goodness and mercy. As I pursue new adventures, I pray that I will not be hasty in making decisions that will impact my business, but allow Your wisdom to guide me.

Amen

Psalms 5:1-3

"Give ear to my words, O Lord,
Consider my meditation.
Give heed to the voice of my cry,
My King and my God, For to You I
will pray. My voice You shall hear
in the morning, O Lord;
In the morning I will direct it to
You, And I will look up."

Have you ever been talking to your friends or even family members, and gotten the impression that they are not really listening to you? Of course you have.

You are pouring out your most intimate thoughts and feelings to them and they are acting as if you are just rambling about the most insignificant thing ever. No need to fear, for God is always listening to our ramblings.

You see, when we have proclaimed Him to be our King, he is always listening. When you meditate and pray (they go hand-in-hand), He is forever ready to hear our voices. In turn, we too must be ready to hear His voice.

What better time to hear him than in the morning! In the minutes after awakening from your slumber, before the business of the world begins to cloud your mind with the swarm of things that must be accomplished, morning prayer should be part of the routine. When your mind is fresh, your attitude is positive, and your mind has been revived by sleep.

∽

Most Gracious Father, I come meditating and praying to You this morning before I allow the business of my day to take over my thoughts. Lord, You are my King and my God, I will forever praise Your name. I am so thankful that when I speak, when I pour out my heart to You, You are always listening. Not only do I cry out to You, I will patiently look toward the heavens as I wait to hear from You.

Amen

Psalms 119:62

*"At midnight I will rise
to give thanks to You,
Because of Your righteous judgments."*

It's midnight and you are still awake. That makes you a night owl, so they say. Truth be told, if you are awake at midnight, you are an early bird, for a new day has begun.

Does it really matter what we call it? No. What matters the most is that you are awake and now is the perfect time to give thanks unto God for His many blessings.

∾

Lord God, I rise and fall to my knees to give thanks to You for all that You have done for me. You have blessed me, my family, my friends, my enemies, and my business, and I say, "Thank You." You have been justified in Your decisions of how and when to bless me and my business, and I say, "Thank You."

Amen

DILIGENCE

"I never could have done what I have done without the habits of punctuality, order, and diligence, without the determination to concentrate myself on one subject at a time."

~ Charles Dickens

Proverbs 10:4

---

*He who has a slack hand becomes poor,
but the hand of the diligent makes rich.*

One of the most difficult tasks for you, the entrepreneur, especially in the beginning, is being or becoming diligent. By definition the word diligent means to be steady, earnest, and putting forth an energetic effort. In the beginning, we are so excited about the prospect of owning a business that we can call our own. Some of you have dreams and aspirations to change the world with your product or service.

As the days, weeks, and months progress, the excitement begins to fade as the weight of what we have embarked upon begins to bare down on us. Between making cold calls, networking, and actually servicing your clients/customers, life as you have known it is no more.

You are up early and getting to bed late, only to toss and turn as you think of all the things that did not get done. Hours are spent in the car between appointments and meetings. Your eating habits consist of fast food and anything filled with caffeine. There has been little time for family and friends. Your social life IS non-existent.

Do not fear!

Because you have been diligent in your business dealings, treating customers with respect and fairness, because you have kept the faith and placed God first in all that you have done, and because you have not been ashamed to share the Gospel as you went about your busy days, God has and will continue to give you the desires of your heart. Your business has and will continue to grow, making you rich in faith and in good works.

∽

Our Father, who art in heaven, I have been diligent in my affairs, never wavering from my true purpose in You. For that, You have given me the desires of my heart and I am truly grateful. On this day, let me be mindful of those around me. Allow my actions to serve as a beacon of light to those who may be lost. When I am tired and frustrated, let me remember why I started this business. And in that moment allow me to become excited and energetic all over again.

AMEN!

II Peter 1:5-9

But also for this very reason,
giving all diligence,
add to your faith virtue to
virtue knowledge,
to knowledge self-control,
to self-control perseverance,
to perseverance godliness,
to godliness brotherly kindness,
and to brotherly kindness love.

For if these things are yours and abound,
you will be neither barren nor unfruitful in
the knowledge of our Lord Jesus Christ.

For he who lacks these things is
shortsighted, even to blindness,
and has forgotten that he was
cleansed from his old sins.

So many times we are reading God's Word and are not able to grasp the context or the meaning of the words being used. To make sure we are all on the same page, let us come to a consensus with the following terms and definitions found in today's scripture.[1]

Faith = Complete trust or confidence

Virtue = A particular moral excellence

Knowledge = Intellectual understanding, personal experience, emotion, and personal relationship

Self-control = A sober, temperate, calm, and dispassionate approach to life, having mastered personal desires and passions

Perseverance = Maintaining Christian faith through the trying times of life

Godliness = An attitude and style of life that acknowledges God's claims on human life and seeks to live in accordance with God's will

Brotherly kindness = To treat others with a steadfast love that maintains relationships through gracious aid in times of need

Love = Unselfish, loyal, and benevolent concern for the well-being of another

If you follow the promptings of the Holy Spirit, you build a *virtuous* character, which builds *knowledge* and wisdom as we seek guidance from the Word of God.

With this knowledge comes the ***self-control*** of your emotions when conducting business. As your ability to control your emotions grows, you will be able to ***persevere*** through the tough times when things are not progressing as you would prefer. We have all heard the saying that life is 10% of what happens and 90% of how we handle it. When you push through those difficult times with a ***godly*** attitude you will be able to approach your ***brother*** with a level of ***kindness*** that surpasses all understanding of the corrupt world in which we live, showing the world that the ***Love*** of Christ will consistently shine through you and your business.

∾

    Lord, it is with open eyes that I can begin to see the fruitfulness of my labor in learning more about You. I am humbled by Your love and kindness towards me, when I have been so undeserving. My prayer is that through You I will continue to be diligent about the business opportunity You have given me.

Amen and Amen.

Proverbs 21:5

---

*The plans of the diligent
lead surely to plenty,
but those of everyone who is hasty,
surely to poverty.*

Have a plan, work the plan.

Have a plan, work the plan.

Have a plan, work the plan.

**Have a plan, consult the manual
(God's Word),
patiently, yet diligently work the plan.**

Whether you have been in business for 1 month or 5 years, planning is one of the many keys to success. From understanding your target customer to deciding on inventory, you, the entrepreneur, have to have a plan of how to reach these goals. Once the goal is established, or once a plan is created, then you have to put the plan into the business timeline for when these goals will be achieved. Notice I said when, not if they are achieved. In December 2014, I became the product of a company lay-off. After a few days of operating in a fog (I truly cannot recall those first few days), I began to develop a plan. This was the first and, I decided, the last time that I would experience something like this. I made a promise to myself that I would stop letting fear stand in the way of working the plan to become a successful business owner. Armed with the personal and professional skills and gifts that I was given, the plan was developed. Every day I am out working the plan. Working the plan means I am doing more networking, more volunteering, more one-to-one meetings with potential clients, and increasing my social media presence.

Now that you are ready to work the plan, realize that some things may not materialize overnight. However, if you work the plan, the blessings of the Lord will surely come.

∽

Master, you have given me the direction that I need to be successful in my business. Thank you for providing me with the manual that gives me focus. I know that if I work the plan according to your purpose that I will be blessed beyond measure.

Thank you, Lord.

II Timothy 2:15

"Be diligent to present yourself approved to God, a worker who does not need to be ashamed, rightly dividing the word of truth."

Let's suppose that you need a line of working capital and you have submitted your application to the bank. The bank has notified you that someone will have to visit your place of business before making a final decision. They are not able to provide an exact date for the visit, because the field officer creates his own timing and schedule.

You arrive at work one morning to find that nothing has been completed to your specifications, an employee has called in sick again, and the city workers have ruptured the water line that runs to your building. While dealing with these issues, a man walks in and announces he is from the bank. You introduce yourself and he says, "It's Me, God."

Would He approve of you in that moment?

Another word comes to mind here as well, *integrity*. Integrity is doing the right thing when no one else is looking. Believe me when I say someone is always looking. They are just waiting for you to not do right. Just remember that they are not the ones you should be concerned about.

Before you make that decision, just ask yourself, "Would God would approve?"

∽

Son of God, You are ever watchful of my goings and my comings. May I always be doing that which I am not ashamed. I ask that you use me as a vessel that is diligently providing the word of truth to those around me.

Amen and Amen

HARD WORK

"Nothing ever comes to one that is worth having, except as aresult of hard work."

~ Booker T. Washington

Ecclesiastes 2:24

Nothing is better for a man than

*that he should eat and drink,
and that his soul
should enjoy good in his labor.
This also, I saw,
was from the hand of God.*

As sole proprietors we often say or hear others saying that there are not enough hours in the day to accomplish everything that needs to be done. Yet at the same time if we are being honest with ourselves, we are not being as productive as we could be. We welcome distractions from the very things that will bring success to our businesses. Using one reason or another as to why we are not laboring to the best of our abilities.

More stock is put into entertaining potential clients than the hard work that is required to keep the client once he/she has been attained. Are you making certain that your product or service is the best that it can possibly be? Are you researching ways to improve your business? Have you explored partnerships that will enhance your business?

When we have spent so many hours, days, weeks, and months working our business, we tend to lose sight of the fact that the success of our business is a gift from God; a gift that should be appreciated and one to be thankful for; a gift that is not to be placed on a shelf to collect dust. The gift of hard work is to be shared with others just as you would share your favorite meal, savoring every morsel to the last bite.

∽

Father, I pray for the strength to continue to labor long and hard for the success of my business. And when my hard work reaps the blessings given by You, I will be mindful to share the fruits of my labor with others.

Amen

James 2:24

You see then that a man is justified by works, and not by faith only.

Faith and works go hand-in-hand. Together they create a bond that is extremely difficult to pull apart. Having the faith that you are competent to have a successful business produces a level of work that is immeasurable in the eyes of onlookers. Work produces maturity and knowledge that propels you to complete what you have started.

It has been my experience when people can see the efforts that you are putting into your business, they are more likely to believe and trust in what you have to offer. They have faith that if they conduct business with you, that you will supply them with what they need. When you perform above and beyond to meet this need, when you exceed expectations, a bond is created that cannot be easily broken.

However first, you must have faith in yourself and what you do. Maybe we should call this self-confidence? Or do we call it skill? It matters not what you call it, as long as you have faith that the gifts and talents that have been given to you by God will serve as the foundation for your successful business.

～

Dear Lord, I desire to be faithful and obedient to You and what You desire of me in this world. I pray that my commitment and hard work for the building of Your kingdom will also manifest in my business. As such, I have faith that I will be rewarded the desires of my heart.

Amen

Psalms 90:16-17

Let Your work appear to Your servants, And Your glory to their children. And let the beauty of the Lord our God be upon us, And establish the work of our hands for us;

Yes, establish the work of our hands.

Upon purchasing a new home a few years ago I became a huge fan of HGTV and DIY Network. After all of the features from the builder, the house still needed to have my personal touch so that we could consider it our home. With time on my hands as a stay-at-home parent, I began watching shows that taught me how to do things around the house for myself. Many of these tasks I was able to complete alone, yet there were some that required help. Thus, I enlisted the labor of my older children. The list is too long to share here, but let's just say that I could open a new business as a basic home repair person (and I have contemplated doing just that).

As each task was completed, I would step back and marvel at the beauty that was being created in our home. Beauty created at the hands of myself and my children. Is that not what we are given every day by our Lord and Savior? We find beauty in nature, the birds singing and the flowers blooming. There is beauty in the sun, the moon, and the stars. There is beauty in the faces of the people we meet every day. Our hands too are creating beauty as we do business, the beauty of hard work that can be shared with our children and their children for years to come.

Society will do its best to convince us that there is no beauty in hard work; that we should all be striving to accomplish the same thing(s), and looking out for ourselves; teaching us and our children that easy is the only way to go; attempting to convey the message that we must all have the same concept of what beauty looks like. Yet, for you and me as believers, we recognize that there is beauty in all things, which allows us to work feverishly to re-create beauty in all that we do, not for our sake, but for the sake of others as we give glory to God.

∽

Lord our God, open my eyes to see the beauty in what I do as an entrepreneur. Help me to recognize that even though I may be temporarily blinded to its beauty, that others see Your hands guiding my hands at work to create that which is pleasing to You. Creating a beauty that is, and will be, visible for years to come.

Amen

II Thessalonians 3:11

For we hear that there are some who walk among you in a disorderly manner, not working at all, but are busybodies.

Thomas A. Edison said,

"Being busy does not always mean real work.
The object of all work is production or accomplishment
and to either of these ends there must be forethought, sys-
tem, planning, intelligence, and honest purpose, as well as
perspiration. Seeming to do is not doing."

Are you always doing something?

Does this activity yield you positive results for your business?

At the end of your day, can you list the things that you
accomplished that were productive?

∽

If you said no to any of those, you may just be a busybody. And if your business is not where you thought it
would be by now, it's likely that deep down inside you
already knew this. Right? Before you say it, yes, I know
you are always doing something, always on the go, and
always networking. However, the question is, "Are these
activities leading to new clients, repeat clients, or increased cash flow?" If not, you may be working in such
a disorderly manner that nothing is ever truly getting
accomplished.

The challenge is to change the behavior of how
you work. Perhaps that means that you begin to make

to-do lists for each day. Maybe you need to re-write (I hope you have them already) your short term or long term goals. By doing this, you can focus your attention on the activities that need to be completed in a timely fashion. Defining and/or prioritizing what is important is crucial to being able to use your time effectively.

ᴄᴏ

Dear Lord, I no longer wish to be a busybody in my business or my spiritual life. Help me to focus on those things that are important to You first, and have the faith to believe that from there everything else will follow suit.

Amen

CHARACTER

"Waste no more time arguing about what a good man should be.
Be one."

~ Marcus Aurelius

Matthew 5:3-12

Blessed are the poor in spirit,
for theirs is the kingdom of heaven.
Blessed are those who mourn,
for they will be comforted.
Blessed are the meek,
for they will inherit the earth.
Blessed are those who hunger and thirst
for righteousness, for they will be filled.
Blessed are the merciful,
for they will be shown mercy.
Blessed are the pure in heart,
for they will see God.
Blessed are the peacemakers,
for they will be called sons of God.
Blessed are those who are persecuted
because of righteousness,
for theirs is the kingdom of heaven.
Blessed are you when people insult you,
persecute you and falsely say all kinds
of evil against you because of Me.
Rejoice and be glad, because great is your
reward in heaven, for in the same way they
persecuted the prophets who were before you.

The word "beatitude" comes from the Latin *beatitudo*, meaning "blessedness." The phrase "blessed are" in each of the beatitudes above implies a current state of happiness or well-being. The beatitudes come from the opening verses of the famous Sermon on the Mount delivered by Jesus where he teaches of the blessings that will be bestowed upon each person who possesses this inner character.

What does your character say about you? Are customers/clients referring others to you based on how you treated them? Are you the walking definition of integrity? Are you treating others the way you would want to be treated? Basically, how are your customer service skills?

The steps of a good man, or woman, are ordered by the Lord and he or she continuously seeks the Lords' guidance.

ᵔᵔ

Eternal Father, I desire to be more Christ-Like. I need You to order my steps so that the path You have purposed for me to travel will be a beacon unto others. I hunger and thirst for Your love. Father, I thank You for creating in me the desire to walk right, the desire to live a life that is good and feels good.

It Is So.

EMPLOYER/EMPLOYEE

"Pride adversely affects all our relationships - our relationship with God and His servants, between husband and wife, parent and child, employer and employee, teacher and student, and all mankind."

~ Ezra Taft Benson

Jeremiah 22:13

Woe to him who builds his house by unrighteousness and his chambers by injustice, who uses his neighbor's service without wages and gives him nothing for his work.

A s I was reading this scripture again and determining how I would tie it into today's devotion, I am reminded of my mother's neighbor. You see, my elderly mother, who lives alone, does not venture out of her yard to cross the street to check her mailbox. Mom's mobility is limited. So every day, her neighbor checks her mail and brings it up to the house for her. On most days, it also becomes a time of day where they engage in conversation.

In this challenging (trying to be nice) world that we live in, Ms. S is in no way obligated to assist my mother in such a manner. By all standards, she is performing a service, of which one would expect to be paid. Yes, we have offered to pay her for helping out, but she refuses to accept any monetary rewards.

So what is the solution? We pay her in other ways. We make sure that when she needs something, if we can help, we do. On special occasions and holidays, we provide her with treats and goodies (we like to cook). And of course, we keep her and her family lifted up in prayer.

There will be times when people will bless you and expect nothing in return for their work or service. Yet, when that same person deserves to be compensated, do not hesitate to do so. Many have been credited with the quote that says,

> "People may not remember exactly what you did, or what you said, but they will always remember how you made them feel."

Be mindful of how you compensate others for the work that is done on your behalf. Whether it is an employee or a client who refers you to others, make them feel good about what they have done by recognizing them for their acts of righteousness and kindness.

∽

Lord, You are righteous and just in all things. Help me to be an imitator of You in my dealings with my employees. Guide my actions, as I seek to make them feel worthy of praise and special in Your eyes.

Thank you, Lord!

Leviticus 19:13

You shall not cheat your neighbor, nor rob him. The wages of him who is hired shall not remain with you all night until morning.

A nyone who knows me well, knows that relationships and how we care for them is near and dear to my heart. We have relationships with the butcher at the local grocery store. We have relationships with the service provider at the dry cleaners. We have relationships with our neighbors. Sometimes these relationships go terribly wrong, usually when one tries to rob the other.

Here is an example:

I reside in a duplex. I share a wall and a garage with my neighbors. Shortly after my neighbors moved in, I came to realize I would not be living next door to Ward and June Cleaver. In the first few months, they had several parties, blocked my portion of the driveway on numerous occasions, and almost burned down the house. I know you are asking how did that last part happen. I am glad that you asked.

One evening upon leaving my dwelling, I noticed that one of those orange heavy duty extension cords had been plugged into an outlet in the garage and it was stretching across the sidewalk into their kitchen door. Not understanding what was happening, I tried to dismiss this action. The next day, as I was working at the computer, I began to smell something burning. The kids who were still in bed, being lazy, noticed the smell too. I walked through the house and nothing seemed to be out of the norm.

I then remembered the extension cord that was exposed to the outside elements (did I mention it is the winter season). I grabbed a thin sweater and headed outside to find that there was smoke coming from the neighbor's kitchen door. As I am frantically making my kids and the dog of what's going on next door, I am also on the phone with the 911 operator and pounding on my neighbors' door. Emergency responders were there within minutes. We are rushed across the street, not properly dressed for the weather, away from our home, praying that everything will be alright. Thankfully things did turn out for the best.

You see my neighbors did not have any power, so they were robbing **me** by plugging into an outlet that was feeding off of the electrical meter to my home. When their power was turned off, they had been cooking and forgot to turn off the burner on the electric stove. When the power was restored that cold and breezy morning, there was an electric skillet that had been placed on that burner and it was ablaze.

I will not mention all of the remaining events of that morning. I will only say that by the grace of God, we were saved from something that could have been a lot worse.

You see when we attempt to rob people in our business dealings or when we rob our neighbors, there are always consequences to our actions. Just as when we rob God there are consequences. When a person has worked for your, you are legally and morally obligated to pay them. If you have been fair in the wages paid to this person, others will see that and will return in kind with their dealings with you. Likewise, the persons being paid, will recognize you as a person of character, who is striving to be more Christ-like.

∽

Holy One, help me to be clear in my relationships with my employees. I strive to be like you, by loving them, and rewarding them for work that has been performed. My action and choices have consequences. Thank you for teaching me how to do act accordingly through the continuous reading and studying of your word.

Amen

III John 1:8

We therefore ought to receive such, that we might be fellow helpers to the truth.

Visit any dating site or ask a single person what is one of the most important characteristics they believe is needed in a relationship and they will say *trust*. Yet, it is possibly the one thing that we no longer do. We are giving power to past hurts by letting them keep us from trusting others. Gone are the days that people trust words, today they trust actions.

Do your employees trust what you do? Do they know that in a pinch, you will chip in and help when needed? Are they watching you and wandering why they work for you?

The people that you work with need to know that you can be trusted. In this chaotic world, they need to know that you will always do the right thing on their behalf.

Father, you are a present help in my times of trouble and I thank You. I pray that I too can be the helper that is needed by those I work with. I ask that my actions will speak when my words cannot. I trust You, Lord, and I pray that those around me, can see that evidence. Shine through me so that others might come to know You as I do.

∽

Thank You, Lord

Nehemiah 3:5

Next to them the Tekoites made repairs; but their nobles did not put their shoulders to the work of their Lord.

Do not ask others to do what you are not willing to do yourself. **Period.**

As a ministry leader in my spiritual community, I find that I am consistently asking others to attend certain meetings. These meetings often include bible study, corporate prayer services, and leadership trainings. The typical response is one where people express that they do not see the benefit of attending such things. These are the times that I find myself sharing how my faith is stronger and how my knowledge was expanded due to my participation in such events. Even on days where I too would rather be somewhere else, I am there, hopefully providing the example they need me to be.

For example, at a community sponsored event to celebrate the 4th of July, I was originally scheduled to volunteer at a booth for a non-profit. The celebration included food, drinks, games, and music. Shortly before the festivities started, I was asked to relocate to a game booth because we were short-staffed. I spent the next 4 hours chasing basketballs and tennis balls in 90-plus degree heat. Inwardly, I was struggling all the way, yet by the end of my shift, I had made kids and adults smile. That was more than enough to make up for being given an otherwise undesirable task in that heat.

As a leader, I am always aware that others are watching me. While they were not the reason I agreed to change booths (I'd have done it anyway), I do know that the next time I ask someone else to step into a less-than-desirable task for me, I will have already shown them my willingness and earned their trust.

༒

Yahweh, You were willing and did do all of those things that You commanded us to do as mere men. It is my desire that I do the same. I will set the standard by working alongside my employees. For we are one in the workings of this business and of You, our Lord and Savior.

Amen

FAIRNESS

"These men ask for just the same thing, fairness, and fairness only. This, so far as in my power, they, and all others, shall have."

~ Abraham Lincoln

Ezekiel 33:17

---

*Yet the children of your people say,
'The way of the Lord is not fair.'
But it is their way which is not fair!*

More often than not, we are quick to say that the next person is not being fair to us in our dealings with them. Perhaps we have heard of some deal of concessions they have made for another person, and we believe that we too deserve that same treatment. We do not bother to ask questions concerning why we are not afforded the same treatment. We assume (and you know the saying that goes with that word), that the person is being difficult or unfair.

Hold up the mirror to yourself and realize that you are the one not being fair in your thoughts and actions toward your fellow business owner or worse, your employee. Unless you have complete knowledge and understanding of how and why a situation has occurred, you truly have no right to demand the same treatment. It could also be that you do not need to be treated in the same manner. You are special in your own right and maybe, just maybe,

God has a better plan for you. Examine your ways and be absolutely certain that you are being fair in everything that you do.

Lord, in all that I do and say, let me be fair. Help me to be cognizant of how I am treating those around me. Let me not assume that I am due the same treatment as others. *I AM SPECIAL* and You have special plans for me. Thank You for the employees and business partners that are just as eager to help make my business successful.

∽

Hallelujah and Amen!

Luke 16:10

---

*He who is faithful in what is least
is faithful also in much;
and he who is unjust in what is
least is unjust also in much.*

Ask any person the question, "Are you selfish?" The most likely answer that you will receive is no. But aren't we all just a little bit selfish when it comes to the things that we want? And that is alright, until it gets out of control and all that you are concerned about *is* self. Yet, I would venture to say that the person who is the least concerned about themselves is also the person who is most generous toward others.

It is crucial that we make the distinction between selfishness and self-care. Selfishness is defined as being concerned, sometimes excessively or exclusively, for oneself or one's own advantage, pleasure, or welfare, *regardless of others*. Self-care is personal health maintenance. It is any activity of an individual with the intention of improving or restoring physical or mental health, or treating or preventing disease.

In my personal life, I have learned that taking care of myself, being fair to myself in my wants and desires only makes me a better person in my service to God, a better mother, and a better business-woman. I have found that things go better when I am faithful to God first and then myself.

We all have people in our lives that we will go above and beyond for because of our relationship with them. But we have to be careful. It was a difficult realization that I could not be all things to all people. When I seek to do that, I am not being fair to them or to myself.

Listen, I know you want to be able to work with everyone, but let's be honest: not everyone is seeking to work with you, to uplift you and your business. They are simply along for the awesome journey that has been given to you.

I keep seeing this posting online that says something like, "You can't tell your dreams to everyone, because they would not understand." I say your dream is not for them to understand. The reciprocal relationship is for you to be faithful, authentic, dutiful, obedient, and just to those who have been placed in your life to bring the dream to reality.

❧

Father in Heaven, If I am faithful and just over a few things, I know that You will give me the desires of my heart. Give me the strength to know and accept when I cannot be all things to all people. First and foremost, I am your servant and as such I strive to be dutiful over my activities in my dealings with others. It is in your holy name that I pray and ask all things.

So Be It

Proverbs 11:1

Dishonest scales are an abomination to the Lord, but a just weight is His delight.

A bomination means an intense aversion or loath-ing; detestation. If we back up to Proverbs 6:16-19[2], we see that there are seven things that are detestable to God; yes, seven are an abomination to Him:

- ✓ A proud look

- ✓ A lying tongue

- ✓ Hands that shed innocent blood

- ✓ A heart that devises wicked plans

- ✓ Feet that are swift in running to evil

- ✓ A false witness who speaks lies

- ✓ And one who sows discord among brethren

༈

As Inge Anderson[3] points out in her blog posting,

> "Dishonest business practices are named as an 'abomination' in Deuteronomy 25: 13-16 KJV, Proverbs 11:1 KJV and Proverbs 20:10 KJV. It seems that scrupulously honest business practic-es are required of any professing to be the Lord's people."

Nothing is more pleasing to God than fair and honest interactions, or more necessary to make us and our devotion acceptable in His eyes.

Every relationship is built on a level of trust and

honesty. As a Diana Gabaldon *Outlander*[4] fan, there is a line in the book/TV series where the main male character says to the main female character that when she tells him something, to let it be the truth. People do not expect you to be dishonest with them, and when you make the mistake of doing so, the relationship is never the same. That is assuming that the relationship continues at all.

Are you being honest with your customers, your vendors, your employees, yourself? If not, why have you chosen this path? What do you hope to gain from being dishonest?

～

Dear Lord, forgive me for my dishonesty toward You, others, and myself. I now know that You are sickened by my behavior. I pray that as I devote myself to Your word, I will notice when my words or actions are not acceptable in Your sight.

Amen

Psalm 112:5

A good man deals graciously and lends; He will guide his affairs with discretion.

A difficult lesson for me to learn has been that not everyone will handle their affairs or appreciate how I handle my affairs. What I mean is that not *everyone* will understand why they do not know *everything* about you or your business.

Allow me to take this a step further. I have a family member, with whom I have chosen not to share things about my business. I made this decision because each time I shared something with them it was immediately shared with other people. The things that this person thinks they know are obtained from the minuscule postings found on social media by her children.

Yes, I have spoken to them about it, and the behavior continues. Therefore, I was forced to make the decision to not share certain information. When they attempt to question me about things that have been shared on social media, I graciously explain the state of affairs around that subject. This means that they receive what I like to call "surface information". In other words, I use *discretion.*

Before you say it, yes, this is family. However, as I am sure that you have learned since starting your business, some people - family members or not - **need** to be kept at bay.

∾

Holy One, thank You for giving me the gracious spirit that guides my affairs. As You order my steps, I am grateful that I am able to handle all things with the utmost level of discretion. I pray that as my faith in You grows that I will continuously be reminded to treat others as I would to be treated.

Amen

DELEGATE

*"I either delegate something,
I dump it, or I deal with it."*

~ Daniel L. Doctoroff

Exodus 18:18

*Both you and these people
who are with you
will surely wear yourselves out.
For this thing is too much for you;
you are not able to perform it
by yourself.*

After struggling to do everything myself, for a number of reasons, I have come to the conclusion that I cannot do all of this work by myself. If I want to be a successful business owner I have to accept that it will need others and their talent to make this happen.

If you are just starting out, assemble a team now that will be able to assist you when the time comes. In order to accomplish this, you must first define your own strengths and weaknesses. After you complete this task, the next step would be to decide what you will need each person to contribute. I caution you here to not just say what you need, but to also explain your vision AND your expectations.

"But I cannot afford to have employees just yet," you might think.

There are other options:

- Look for students to work as interns

- Students may also be looking for options to complete a project for a particular subject

- Seek out volunteers who believe in what you are doing

- Barter services with another business owner

These are just a few of the options you may want to consider when assembling your team.

Burnout can occur quickly if we are not careful. The long hours will come, so I challenge you to use that time building your brand and leaving other tasks to your team.

⤳

Lord of Lords, I need help. I am only one person and I cannot do it all. Please direct me toward those who will share the vision that You have given me for this business. I pray that the team members will be able to work individually and collectively for the greater good.

Amen

Psalms 33:9

For He spoke, and it was done;
He commanded, and it stood fast.

I am the youngest of four children for my parents. Growing up, when my mother said to do something, it was done. No hesitation, no questions, no nothing. Unfortunately, as I matured into a young adult, that did not change much. I simply did what I was told to do.

Through some of life's experiences, I began understanding that if I continued on this path, I would not be happy with myself. Even after this realization, it took me a while to move out of my pattern of behavior for a number of reasons, primarily: fear. This internalized fear turned into anxiety and depression.

But then I remembered something that I once read which said *fear* was simply **F**alse **E**vidence **A**ppearing **R**eal. What I was afraid of was all a state of mind, and it could be replaced with positive thoughts and actions.

Let me just say that this was not an easy task for me and I am almost certain it will not be easy for some of you either. Yet, I was determined to not allow this un-welcome presence continue to take up space in my mind for free. I recalled that the voices that had been speaking were not that of God, and I began crying out to God. Over time, I began hearing a different voice, His voice telling me that I had nothing to fear, for He was with me. He began to speak and things started happening.

When God speaks to you for your business or your personal life there is nothing that can stop you from accomplishing what He has already purposed for you. Cry out to Him from your heart and ask for what you need. Seek Him and it will be done.

∽

Oh God, I call out to You today for what I need to overcome this fear that is present in my mind. You have not given me this spirit of fear, so I know that I can over-come this obstacle. Lord, when You speak, it is done and I praise You for that.

Praise the Lord, Amen

Matthew 21:6

So the disciples went and did as Jesus commanded them.

Recently I joined a fraternal organization to appease my mother. This group has been in existence for over 100 years. Its historical foundation is one that appeals to me on a personal and a spiritual level. With that being said, there is one aspect of the tradition that bothers me: not questioning directives that have been given by the elders.

At this point of my life, I should have known better than to think that I would be willing to blindly be led by someone else, without the benefit of being able to ask for clarification.

If you are a new business owner with employees, you cannot delegate tasks to them without allowing them to ask for clarification. This allows them to gain an understanding of what and/or how things need to be done.

If you have proven your worth, as Jesus had already done with the disciples, there is a low probability for the need of clarification. Your team has established a history with you and they know what you expect. Therefore, they are more than willing to do those things that have been delegated by you without question.

∾

Most High God, I am ready to do as You have commanded. Whatever it is that You need me to do, I will do without question. Wherever You need me to go, I will go. And Lord, I thank You in advance for guiding me through this rugged terrain of life and business. I thank You for being my guiding compass. In the blessed name of Jesus, I pray…

Amen

2 Chronicles 35:2

And he set the priests in their duties and encouraged them for the service of the house of the LORD.

I have been blessed in my professional career to have had bosses who allowed me to be independent in my daily work. They were not micromanagers, except one. This person would delegate a task to me and then question and micromanage everything that I did to accomplish the task. Unlike Josiah, who assigned the priests their duties and encouraged them in their work and their service, this boss was not equipped to do either.

Can you recall such a person in your life? Did you enjoy working with that person as they peered over your shoulder? Are you that type of boss?

Telling employees what to do is the easy part of being the boss. The more difficult skill to master is how to positively encourage and empower those same people to work confidently. Early on, when you are establishing those working relationships, you have to take the necessary time to learn how to not only to be a successful boss, but also the type of leader that your employees or others are thrilled to work with.

∾

Lamb of God, I need You to instruct me on how to be the kind of boss and leader that is pleasing to You. You embody the persona of the best leader ever, and I desire to be more like You. With Your guidance, Lord, I am confident that I will be able to delegate others to be their best. In the name of Jesus,

Amen

REST

"Rest and be thankful."

~ William Wordsworth

Exodus 23:12

*Six days you shall do your work,
and on the seventh day you shall rest,
that your ox and your donkey may rest,
and the son of your female servant
and the stranger may be refreshed.*

Growing up as a child in the south, Sundays were special days in our household. It was the day that we went to church, of course, and then the remainder of the day was spent with family. Either we were visiting someone or we were at home enjoying each other. Dinner was always a 10 course meal, or at least that's what it seemed to be. And then you rested.

You Rested!

There was no doing laundry or going to the grocery store. You did not go shopping because retailers were closed, so that they too could rest. There were no little league soccer or softball games or practice. It was a day of rest.

As a business owner, we have grown accustomed to working non-stop; hardly ever taking the time to rest. As my daughter would say, "The grinding never stops." Yet, if the grinding never stops, how do we replenish the most powerful part of our bodies, our minds?

Before you say it, I already know that psychologically and physically the body (including the mind) replenishes itself each night as we sleep. But I also know that you are likely only sleeping maybe four to six hours each night. So in essence, the mind really is not recuperating.

I love Sundays. I still go to church to worship and praise God. The good news is that once I am home, I am in rest-mode. I figure out dinner, get into my comfy clothing, and rest. No laundry, no working at the computer, no nothing. I have even gotten into the habit of taking a nap. My kids think this makes me old. Whatever!

After six days of working and one day of rest, on Monday I am ready to conquer the world.

∽

Master, I promise that I will take heed to Your word. I will rest my whole body so that I may be energized and focused to be in service to You. Lord, thank You for giving me this body, and I vow to take care of it to the best of my ability, starting today, by resting in the comfort of Your word.

Amen

Psalms 127:2

It is vain for you to rise up early, to sit up late, and to eat the bread of sorrows; for so He gives His beloved sleep.

I have reached the age that an alarm clock no longer takes up space on my beside table. No matter the day of the week, my body wakes around the same time. This can be a bit frustrating when one would rather stay under the covers and sleep the day away. It has been some years since this behavior began, but it's just the way it has become. Even though I am usually out of bed early, I am back in bed at what I would like to call a decent hour. Meaning, it is a rare occasion that you will find me up past 10:00pm. I am the person who needs eight hours of sleep in order to be semi-functioning the next day. When I do not get my full seven to eight hours, I am grumpy, can't focus, and usually have to take a "power" nap.

Recently, I read an article in **Inc.** magazine[5] that warned leaders about not getting the proper amount of sleep. It stated four things that could occur if one is not careful:

1. Memory loss

2. Concentration problems

3. Increased appetite

4. Depression

Of course, these are just a few possibilities of how the body reacts when it is deprived of sleep.

I do realize that we are not the same; you have to know how much rest works for you. You are in control of your schedule. You decide what needs to be done and what can wait. Not everything can be completed in one day. We have to prioritize, make lists (if that's what you do), and move forward. Even the Lord says to stop trying to burn the candle at both ends, for it is in vain.

∽

Holy One, help me to prioritize my day so that I may be able to rise and fall when appropriate for what You have planned for me. You are my strength and I will rise early to spend time with You, before my external environment has a chance to sway my daily progress.

Amen

Exodus 16:23

Then he said to them,
"This is what the Lord has said:
'Tomorrow is a Sabbath rest, a holy
Sabbath to the Lord.
Bake what you will bake today,
and boil what you will boil;
and lay up for
yourselves all that remains,
to be kept until morning.'"

I am blessed to have a second mother and father. Not because of any particular situation or circumstance. Simply because they are special to me and I get treated like one their one children.

A few weeks ago, I was visiting their home on a Sunday afternoon. I arrived in the middle of dinner. Of course, I had no plans to eat, but was reminded that it is disrespectful to arrive during a meal and not eat. As I grabbed a plate, I noticed all the food on the table. On the table was a green salad, steamed broccoli, green beans, cornbread, rice, and baked pork. And these were not small dishes of food. There was enough food for at least eight people to be served very healthy portions, but that is just how this family operates. You see, I know that "Mother" probably spent the better part of Saturday preparing this food so that when she got home on Sunday, only a few dishes needed to be finished.

Gone are the days when our mothers and grand-mothers cooked on Saturday so that on the Sabbath after service, they could rest and enjoy the family. Gone are the days that we display our food in a formal fashion and serve ourselves and our guests with the good china. We need days like that again.

As a Christian, I recognize the Sabbath day as Sunday. Nonetheless, no matter your faith or the religion you practice, the day of rest does exist. Just as we prepare for the six days of work, let us prepare for the one day of rest.

Precious Lord, I have prepared for the Sabbath of rest. I pray that I will purposefully use this day for the renewing of my mind. Just as important, I pray that I will use this day of rest to connect with family and friends in a method that is pleasing unto you.

Amen

Biblical scholars debate that the idea of rest in this scripture refers to the land or place where the children of God were being led by Moses. Moses is tired and he begins to question that which he cannot see. God reassures Moses by telling him that His presence is enough and if he continues to have faith, He will give him rest.

Does that sound familiar?

We work and work and work, just hoping that the goals and plans that we have for our businesses will come true. We have done all of the things that God has told us, and like Moses, we still cannot see our place of rest.

I will take it a step further. We have listened to the supporters and the cynics by doing many of the things they have suggested. We have chartered unfamiliar territory all for the sake of achieving the goal and nothing has materialized.

Jeremiah 29:11 says, "For I know the thoughts that I think toward you, says the LORD, thoughts of peace and not of evil, to give you a future and a hope." Since we hold that this is truth, stand firm on the promises of God. In due time you will be in His presence and it is there that you will find rest.

∽

Messiah, I seek your presence this day as I travel to and fro. I thank You for the ability to see You in all things that surround me. I long to be in Your presence for it is there I will find peace. Father it is in You that I seek rest.

Amen

Matthew 11:28

*Come to Me, all you who labor
and are heavy laden,
and I will give you rest.*

I realize that up until this point I have committed a great injustice against you. I have assumed that if you have been reading this book that you also have a relationship with Jesus Christ. Forgive me for making that assumption.

For those who have been taking this journey with me, I continue to lift you and your business up in the name of Jesus. I pray that he continues to give you increasing abundance, so that you will not only be blessed beyond measure, but that you will also be a blessing unto others.

My friends who may not have a relationship with Him. I invite you to come unto Him, for He will give you rest like no other.

You say, "How can I know that which I cannot see?"

We are surrounded by hundreds of things that we cannot see with the human eye, yet we believe and accept that they exist. We cannot see germs without a microscope, but we know they are real. We cannot see the wind, yet we know it is present by the movement of the trees. We accept that the earth is suspended in the universe, rotating on an axis around the sun.

We cannot see these things, but we can feel them, right?

When life and business has left you weak and bruised, He will strengthen and heal you so that you can continue to run this race of life. When all of those around you have an agenda that is not beneficial to you, He will keep you focused. When finances are tight, He is a provider. When you doubt yourself and are fearful, He is a protector. When you are lonely, He can be your companion. And when you feel that no one loves you, the Bible says that, "For God so loved the world that He gave His only begotten Son, that whoever believes in Him should not perish but have everlasting life. For God did not send His Son into the world to condemn the world, but that the world through Him might be saved" (John 3:16-17).

So I invite you to come unto Him, and He will give you rest. All you have to do is believe within your heart, confess your wrongdoings, and accept Him as your Lord and Savior.

Our Father, who art in Heaven, Hallowed be thy name. Lord, You are such an awesome God! For my friends who know You, I lift them up to You right now, Lord. I pray that if it is Your will, that You will give them the desires of their hearts. Lord, for my friends whose relationships with You may have fallen to the side, I pray that they will rekindle that relationship with You. And for my friends who do not know You, Lord, I pray that something that I have said will compel them to want to know You. I am hoping that the love I poured out in these pages unto You will propel them to seek You out. Thank You, Father, for giving me the wisdom, knowledge, and love to share in these pages. Continue to use me for I know the best is yet to come, and for that I say THANK YOU.

Amen and Amen

Works Cited

1. Brand, Chad, Charles Draper, and Archie England. (2003). *Holman Illustrated Bible Dictionary.* Holman References, Nashville, TN.

2. Proverbs 6: 16-19 reads, "These six things the Lord hates, Yes, seven are an abomination to Him: A proud look, A lying tongue, Hands that shed innocent blood, A heart that devises wicked plans, Feet that are swift in running to evil, A false witness who speaks lies, And one who sows discord among brethren."

3. Anderson, Inge. (1999). *What is an Abomination to God?* Retrieved from www.glow.cc/abomination on June 19, 2015.

4. Gabaldon, Diana. *The Outlander Series.* Scovil, Galen, and Ghosh Literary Agency, Inc. Retrieved from http://www.dianagabaldon.com/resources on June 19, 2015.

5. Triplett, Indigo. (2015). 4 Problems Sleep Deprivation Can Cause. Retrieved from http://www.inc.com on